THE WONDER IN WATER

by Diane Swanson

ANNICK PRESS

TORONTO + NEW YORK + VANCOUVER

ANNICK PRESS LTD.

We acknowledge the support of the Canada Council for the Arts, the Ontario Arts Council, and the Government of Canada through the Book Publishing Industry Development Program (BPIDP) for our publishing activities.

Edited by Elizabeth McLean
Cover design and interior design by Irvin Cheung/iCheung Design

The text was typeset in Celeste and Gill Sans

CATALOGING IN PUBLICATION DATA
Swanson, Diane, 1944–
The wonder in water / Diane Swanson.

Includes index.
ISBN 1-55037-937-2 (bound).—ISBN 1-55037-936-4 (pbk.)

1. Water—Juvenile literature. I. Title.

GB662.3.S93 2005   j553.7 C2005-901277-3

Printed and bound in China

PUBLISHED IN THE U.S.A. BY	**DISTRIBUTED IN CANADA BY**	**DISTRIBUTED IN THE U.S.A. BY**
Annick Press (U.S.) Ltd.	Firefly Books Ltd.	Firefly Books (U.S.) Inc.
	66 Leek Crescent	P.O. Box 1338
	Richmond Hill, ON	Ellicott Station
	L4B 1H1	Buffalo, NY 14205

Visit our website at: www.annickpress.com

CONTENTS

"If there is magic on this planet, it is contained in water."

— Loren Eiseley, NATURALIST AND ANTHROPOLOGIST

SALTY SWEAT

Right this second, sweat is oozing out from glands inside your skin. You have more than 2 million of them all over your body. Like everyone else, you are ALWAYS sweating, even when you don't know you are.

Your sweat is mostly water. So is your blood. In fact, when you were born, your body was nine-tenths water, and you'll still be mainly water when you're grown! Sweat water also contains salt, and some of it has other nutrients, too, such as proteins.

You're lucky that you ooze sweat. It helps to cool you down as it dries on your skin. And it feeds and waters the masses of bacteria—one-celled life forms, or microbes—that live on you. If you peer at your skin through

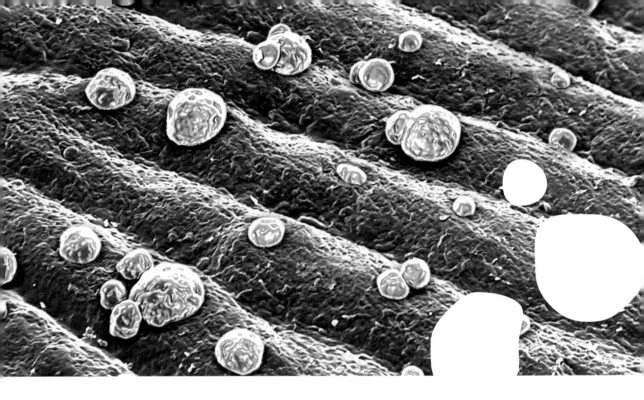

a powerful microscope, you can spot them everywhere. There are about 100,000 on a patch hardly bigger than your smallest fingernail. These bacteria crowd out nasty microbes, keeping them from settling on you and making you sick.

Now and then, little visitors—ladybugs, sweat bees, moths, and butterflies—might land on your skin and dine on the water and salt in your sweat. Some of these insects also feed by sucking sweat out of your tossed-aside T-shirts and sneakers!

From salty sweat to salty seas, there's enough

Beads of sweat—water for bacteria—seep from the skin on a fingertip.

water on this planet to fill 325 million trillion large milk jugs! Some of that water is inside groceries, plants, and animals like you, but almost all of it—about 98 percent—sits in the oceans. Another 1.5 percent is frozen, especially as thick ice at Earth's poles and as mountain glaciers, which are masses of

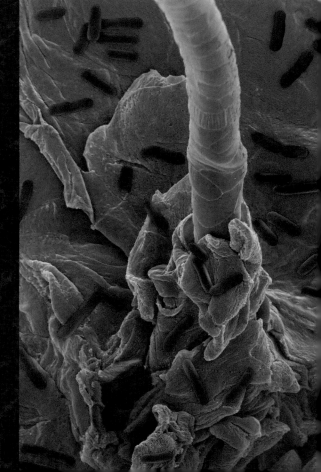

Human sweat can kill the disease-causing bacteria around this hair.

KILLER SWEAT

Sweat water isn't healthy for everything that tries to settle on skin. In fact, it contains an ingredient that's deadly! This ingredient can kill some of the microbes that try to sneak into cuts and infect you—without bothering the good bacteria.

Having killer sweat is great for you, but it's even better for a hippopotamus. This big African beast often gets scratched and wounded in fights, but its sticky red sweat helps destroy disease-causing bacteria. What's more, the sweat is a sunscreen, keeping the almost hairless hippo from burning.

year-round snow and ice. The remaining water makes up the world's clouds, rain, puddles, wetlands, rivers, and lakes.

But whatever form water takes, it supports life right around the planet. Not only does it supply food and moisture, it provides shelter, protection, even transportation. Life as you know it cannot exist without water.

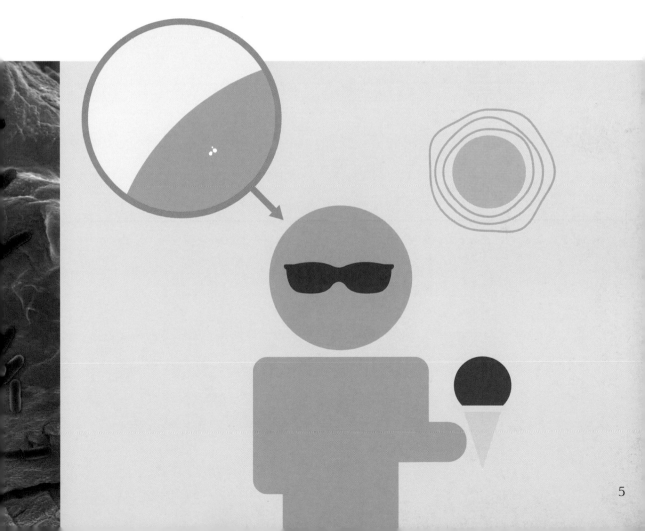

FALLING RAINDROPS

High in the sky, a single raindrop forms from melting ice or snow or from a million cloud droplets all joining together. But as clear as that drop looks when it plunks on your arm, it is more than water. A raindrop needs something inside it—a speck of dust, smoke, salt, even live bacteria—to form and fall. Amazingly, bacteria grow and reproduce in the clouds!

As raindrops fall, they gather bits and pieces of almost everything they touch. They also pick up whole seeds and seedlike spores. And if you look through a microscope, you might discover some one-celled swimmers called amebas (ah-MEE-bahs) in a single drop.

More surprising—but rare—are the little animals that can travel with rain after hurricanes and tornadoes suck them skyward. Trapped inside these powerful, whirling winds, insects, spiders, fish, frogs, and birds can move long distances before rain brings them back to Earth. Sad to say, they usually end up dead.

It's also possible for frozen rain—hailstones—to carry life forms. Swept to

Even freshly fallen raindrops are home to life.

the clouds, they can mix with water droplets and freeze inside the stones. In 1930, scientists reported that a turtle, about the size of a dustpan, had fallen in a frozen ball during a heavy hailstorm in the United States!

Once on Earth, raindrops bring life-giving water to many plants and animals—often by soaking soil, forming puddles, or topping up marshes, lakes, rivers, and oceans. Like you, plants and animals can't survive long without moisture. But some don't even let the rain touch the planet. High in their treetop homes, for instance, great apes called orangutans stick out their tongues to catch raindrops as they fall or lick them off their own hairy coats.

SLITHERING SLIME

Among the weirdest travelers in raindrops and wind are spores from slime molds. After heavy rains, tiny cells creep out of the spores. They eat things such as bacteria and bits of rotting plants. You might see some slime mold cells that have massed together. They form jellylike blobs that slither s-l-o-w-l-y over damp lawn and logs. The distance they cover in an hour is no greater than the width of a wire in a paper clip.

In 1973, a yellow glob of dog vomit slime mold—almost a metre (3 feet) across—moved up a telephone pole in Texas. It scared folks so much they called firefighters to attack it. But even big masses of slime molds don't harm people. When food runs short, the molds just produce more spores, and the cycle begins again.

Rain-delivered slime mold is so freaky it inspired a movie called *The Blob.*

PATCHY PUDDLES

Raindrops with no place to run off or soak in can form puddles. Big and small, they often appear in potholes, ditches, eavestroughs, and birdbaths. You've seen them everywhere, probably even splashed through a few.

Puddles might last only hours, days, or weeks, but until they dry up completely, they help support life of all kinds. Even animals as large as elephants stop to slurp water from them. And many birds use puddles as more than drinking holes. The water is also important for bathing because feathers thick with dirt and pests make it hard for birds to fly and stay healthy.

Jump in a shallow puddle and you might slip

on something slimy—a patch of amebas that have settled on the bottom. The water is likely teeming with them and with other microbes, too. You might also notice a yucky green scum at the puddle's surface. It's probably a mass of algae, life forms that live in water and damp soil. As simple as algae are—many have just one cell—they are important to have around. Besides being food for many animals, they

Like puddles everywhere, puddles in forests help critters survive.

produce much of the world's oxygen!

From algae to bacteria, tiny kinds of life often share the same puddle. Some of them are already living beneath the water when a puddle first forms. Others arrive in raindrops or drift in with the wind.

Small animals that can swim AND jump or walk are also perfect for puddles. That's why skinny scuds—flea-shaped relatives of shrimp and lobsters—are so common there. About as long as mosquitoes, they swim around in the

Spadefoot toad tadpoles try to mature before their muddy puddle dries up.

water, scrounging bits of food from plant and animal wastes. And when a puddle dries up, the scuds simply hop away and find another. No problem.

Where rainfall is rare—in dry plains and deserts—spadefoot toads rush from their moist underground burrows to any freshly formed puddles. There they call out to other toads to come and mate. The female toads lay strings of eggs in the water, and the eggs hatch fast—sometimes in a day!

Young toads, called tadpoles, that emerge from the eggs develop quickly in puddles, usually feeding on floating bits of plants. Some kinds of spadefoot tadpoles grow to become land-living toads in two to three weeks. That's much sooner than bullfrog tadpoles, which take years to mature! But if a puddle is drying up especially fast, some spadefoot tadpoles develop super-sized heads and mouths. Then they eat the others, speeding up their own growth. These special survivors hop away as toads when the puddle is gone.

Landing on a pitcher plant, a mosquito will lay its eggs in a tiny puddle inside.

PITCHER MOSQUITOES

Meat-eating pitcher plants collect rain in trumpet-shaped leaves, forming some of the smallest puddles in the world. Still, pitcher plant mosquitoes lay eggs in them. Although the plants trap some kinds of insects and spiders as food, they don't harm the pitcher plant mosquitoes.

After the eggs hatch, the mosquito larvae live underwater, dining on microbes in the puddles. They might also gobble leftover bits from the animals that the pitcher plants feed on. Some mosquito larvae spend all winter in puddles that freeze solid in the pitcher plant leaves. But as soon as the ice melts, the larvae start moving about and feeding again.

FRESHWATER MARSHES

Even at their driest, freshwater marshes are soggy places—wetlands usually covered by water less than 2 metres (6 feet) deep. You can often find them along rivers and lakes. Fed mostly by rain, snow, and rivers, marshes are bigger than puddles and last much longer. But they're not as constantly wet as lakes.

You're sure to know a freshwater marsh when you pass one. Just look at what's growing there. Along the edges, you'll spot plenty of plants such as cattails that live partly in and partly out of the water. They have a special way of breathing, sending air to their roots through skinny tunnels in their long leaves. You'll also notice water lilies and other plants that float on marsh water. They breathe through openings in the tops of their leaves.

Freshwater marshes are thick with plants—and microbes—partly because the soils beneath them are packed with nutrients. And all that food attracts many kinds of animals. No wonder marshes are fun places to explore. On one visit, you might come across water rodents called muskrats nibbling the cattails, or see river otters diving after frogs that hide in the mud. Another time, you might spot a huge moose as it wades into a marsh to

Tall cattails grow from roots beneath marsh water while small plants float on top.

17

munch water lilies, one of its favorite meals.

Each spring and fall, ducks and other birds that travel long distances use marshes as stopovers—places to rest and feed on their journeys. The ducks especially like to eat duckweed—the smallest flowering plants in the world. With leaves no bigger than match heads, thousands of them can blanket the marsh. They can fool you into mistaking the water for a solid field!

Beneath the surface, fish feast on algae and insects. In turn, they become food for other animals, including wading birds such as herons. When the marshes run dry, some of the fish head for deeper neighboring waters. A few others might burrow in the muddy bottoms of marshes until the water rises again.

Many animals build homes in freshwater marshes. Take the amazing water spider—the only spider that lives completely under water.

A cow moose visits a quiet marsh to graze.

It spins a sheet of silk among plant stems, then uses its hairy back legs to capture air bubbles from the surface. The spider stores the bubbles beneath the silk sheet so it can breathe. Red-winged blackbirds also use marsh plants to set up house, making nests among old brown stems. When the brown-feathered females sit on their eggs, they hide by blending with the color of the stems.

Frequent feeding in a muddy marsh stains the head of a snow goose.

Some muskrats make lodges by heaping cattails and gluing them together with mud. Then they burrow into the mounds and scoop out a room inside each one. Swans often nest on top of these mounds—apartment-style— but the weight soon crushes the lodges beneath. The muskrats are forced to move out and build other homes on the marsh.

RUSTY SNOW GEESE

Loud barking and a flurry of feathers announce the arrival of snow geese at marshes. Traveling between the United States and their arctic breeding grounds, they have to feed well to boost their energy. After all, some snow geese fly as fast as 95 kilometres (60 miles) an hour and cover 1000 kilometres (620 miles) nonstop!

You can tell if the snow geese have been eating lots just by looking at them. With their sharp-edged bills, they poke their heads and necks right into rich marsh mud to chomp plant roots. The iron in the mud turns their snowy white feathers a rusty-orange color.

QUIET LAKES

Surrounded by land, lakes are masses of water—usually fresh—that last year round. Most are filled by rain and snow, rivers, or melting glaciers. Scientists who study these masses of water tend to call them all lakes, no matter what their size. Other people often label smaller ones "ponds." Whatever you call them, you likely think of lakes or ponds as great places to go swimming, diving, and boating as well as to watch wildlife.

At the surface of water, there's a film that's strong enough to support a few lightweight animals. This "surface film"—on any body of water—exists because its smallest particles, called molecules, are so attracted to one another. Each water molecule is more strongly attracted to the water molecules below and next to it than

Don't let a still lake fool you. It's teeming with life, especially in the shallows.

it is to the air molecules above. Hit the water hard when you leap into a lake and you cut right through the surface film. Ouch! Your body lets you know it's there.

Critters that are able to travel across the surface film move in different ways. Fringes of scales on the long toes of lizards called basilisks (BAS-i-lisks) help them stay on top of lakes—as long as they run fast. Whirligig beetles zoom around in the film by stroking the water with wide flat legs edged in hair. If you swish your hand through the film of a lake, you might see these beetles suddenly crowd together, each one whirling in small circles.

Diving birds, such as belted kingfishers, pierce the surface film of lakes or rivers whenever they hunt for food. From as high up as 15 metres (50 feet), the kingfishers plunge steeply—head-first—into the water to seize small fish. Not far under, they slam on the brakes by spreading their wings.

Where sunlight pours into the shallows of lakes, plants thrive, providing plenty of food for animals. But farther from shore, especially in deeper, dimmer parts, life thins out fast. Along the bottom, some fish eat worms in the mud or snatch waste settling down from above. Special feelers help them find their meals in the darkness.

When winter caps the water with ice, lakes look lifeless. But they're not. If a lake still contains oxygen and gets enough light, animals can stay active. If it doesn't, some such as crayfish burrow into the bottom and sleep deeply until spring. Even American

Ever alert, a belted kingfisher spots fish for lunch in a lake below.

alligators can survive in frozen lakes. If the ice locks them in place—with their nostrils above the surface—they simply wait for a thaw to turn them loose.

Life survives INSIDE ice, too. Scientists found microbes in the frozen layers that cover Antarctica's cold lakes. They live in tiny pockets of water trapped within the ice. The microbes seem to make their own

Amazingly, about 60,000 seals live and hunt in the fresh waters of Baikal Lake.

"antifreeze"—like the stuff people put in cars—to keep the pockets of water from freezing.

Furry North American beavers handle cold winters by snuggling inside the lodges they build in lakes. The lodges poke above the surface and have underwater entrances even when the lake is frozen. Made mostly of wood and mud, these houses have fresh-air "vents" in their roofs. Just as you can see your breath on a cold day, you can tell if a family of beavers is at home. Simply watch for warm air vapor rising from a lodge.

BAIKAL WONDERS

Earth's oldest and deepest lake holds one-fifth of the world's fresh water, not counting what's frozen in masses of ice. And it brims with life from top to bottom. Baikal (beye-KAL) Lake in Russia is home to 1500 different kinds of animals and 1000 different kinds of plants. Many of them can't be found anywhere else.

One of the lake's special creatures is the golomyanka (golo-MEE-ahnkah), a fish that travels from depths of 1600 metres (5250 feet) to the surface and back again! No one is sure why it makes these long trips, but at least its super-fat body helps keep the fish warm in deep, cold water.

Another of the lake's unique animals is the Baikal seal, which eats the golomyanka. It's the only seal on the planet that lives in fresh water.

FAST-FLOWING RIVERS

Rain, snow, and melting glaciers create streams of water called rivers, usually in hills or mountains. They can be long or short, wide or narrow, fast or slow. Rivers flow into marshes, lakes, and oceans—or join other rivers. And they change along the way. Charging down a mountain, a narrow river slows as the land levels out. It can widen, too. By the time it reaches an ocean, for instance, it might have turned into a sluggish giant.

Life in slow rivers can be a lot like the life in lakes and freshwater marshes. But surviving in fast-flowing rivers means dealing with the force of the water. Think of river rafting and you'll know how strong that force can be. A swift river can easily whip a raft holding a dozen people, including you, downstream—no rowing needed. Fall in and you'll be swept away!

Hanging on is the challenge to living in swift water. It calls for special features and different

Wild and rocky, a swift river is home only to the animals adapted to its strength.

Up, up, and away!
A river salmon
takes a mighty
leap to the top of
a waterfall.

ways of moving and feeding. The larvae of
little insects called stoneflies, for instance,
cling to the undersides of rocks and let the
water rush over their flattened bodies. As they
nibble on algae, the river pushes them down
instead of lifting them up and away.

Blackfly larvae use rear-end hooks to hang
onto the silk mats that they spin and weave
over rocks. There the larvae filter bacteria and

other bits of food from the swift water. But if they're knocked off the rocks, they depend on their lifelines—slender strands of silk that tie them to the mats. The larvae get back to the rocks by working their way along these lines, eating them up as they go!

Fish such as salmon and trout have streamlined bodies that slip easily through water in rapid rivers. Power-packed muscles propel them—even against the flow—as they catch insects to eat. Some salmon are so strong they can leap up waterfalls as high as 6 metres (20 feet).

A snake-shaped fish called a lamprey uses a big sucker surrounding its mouth to attach itself to river rocks. That way it can rest without getting carried downstream. By gripping stronger fish the same way, the lamprey can hitch rides through the river.

Small songbirds called dippers spend their whole lives in or near swift water. They dine mostly on the tiny insects they find there. Amazingly, the dippers can hold their own in fast rivers. You can spot them swimming or running underwater. With wings always moving, these birds can stay close to the river bottom. Special scales seal their nostrils shut, and a layer of fine down close to their skin keeps them warm in chilly water. To waterproof their thick feather coats, the dippers use oil made by a gland near the base of their tails.

Raccoons sometimes approach fast-flowing rivers to catch fish. Using sharp claws on their back feet, they cling tightly to a bank and reach out with their front feet, trying to snag dinner. In calmer water, they would swim or wade in to hunt, but rapids make them cautious.

Swift rivers can even sweep away animals as large as bears—if they plunge right into the water. But bears that wade among the shallows to fish count on their mighty weight and long claws to hold themselves in place. With mouths open wide, they catch salmon that spring up from the water, or with a single paw, whack a fish from the wild river onto the bank.

New Zealand's blue duck prepares to dive into a fast-moving river.

BLUE DUCK BLUES

One of the birds best suited to fast-flowing rivers is disappearing! For millions of years, the blue duck has lived in New Zealand—and nowhere else. Its blue color helps it hide among wet river rocks. Its streamlined head and large webbed feet help it swim through swift water. And its claws grip boulders tightly while the duck eats insects underwater. Even its upper bill is designed to scrape the insects off rocks.

For years, the number of blue ducks has fallen as more animals hunted them and people changed the rivers where they swam. New Zealanders are now working hard to save them so the only blue ducks won't be the ones pictured on the country's $10 bill.

SALTY SEAS

More life exists in seas, or oceans, than any place else on Earth. That's not too surprising when you consider that they cover about 70 percent of the planet. Still, if you've ever swallowed sea water while swimming or surfing, you'll know it's much saltier than river or lake water. It's also saltier than the body water inside you. In fact, sea water contains enough salt to draw water out of you and many other animals.

Ocean creatures, however, are well adapted to living in salt water. Most sea-drinking fish have cells in their gills that help their bodies get rid of the extra salt they take in. Sea turtles have special glands that expel it, and whales pee it out as a thin paste. The body water inside lobsters and crabs is about as salty as the sea, so they don't need to get rid of salt to keep well.

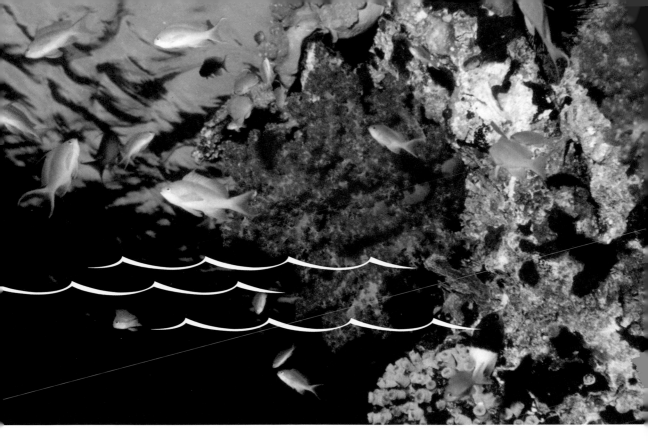

Drifting mostly near the ocean's surface are masses of plankton—microbes and tiny, free-floating plants and animals, including newly hatched fish. You might spot some plankton and think it's just a huge patch of green, yellow, or brown discolored water. But it's actually a rich "pasture," the beginning of many food chains in the ocean.

For instance, plankton animals feed on

Light filtering through water helps make rich homes for sea life, such as fish.

In water too deep for most life, tubeworms thrive near a vent in the sea floor.

plankton plants. Little fish nibble on the plankton animals, then become food for bigger fish. In turn, these fish might be eaten by sea birds that are snapped from the ocean's surface by seals or grabbed on shore by wolves.

Earth's largest beast, the blue whale, is part of the sea's shortest food chain. It grazes directly on the tiny life within plankton. But to fuel its gigantic body—as heavy as 100 cars—the whale strains masses of plankton through bristly plates that hang from its top jaw. Then it licks them off with a tongue that weighs as much as an elephant!

Most sea animals live in water that gets enough light to support plants. In some places, grasses provide food and homes for crabs and snails. And seaweed called bull kelp stands in tall forests—meals for fish and sea urchins, and shelter for animals as big as gray whale calves.

While some of the world's 150 different kinds of octopuses live in shallow water, others tend to stay farther down. They make homes in undersea caves, holes in rocks, even chests in sunken ships. After all, an octopus can slide through any opening big enough for its parrotlike beak—the only hard part in its entire body.

Swordfish usually live far offshore. They're often in water that's close to freezing temperatures, so it's good they have a special heating organ near their eyes. The swordfish can see more clearly when they warm their eyes up. That's especially important when they are hunting speedy squid. Seeing better might also help the swordfish spot its enemy, the big sperm whale—and avoid being swallowed whole!

Survival in the darkest water at the bottom of seas is even harder. So you can imagine their surprise when scientists found steaming-hot water blasting through cracks in the deep ocean floor. Clustered around those vents were giant clams, ghostly white crabs, and tubeworms 1.5 metres (5 feet) long. Their food chain seemed to start—not with plankton—but with a chemical that bacteria use to make food. Just one more wonder in the world of water!

A sea anemone swallows food whole, then spits out what it can't digest.

TIDEPOOL TRICKS

Ocean water flows ashore each day with the rising tides, creating pools—called tidepools—in rocky hollows. These pools are natural aquariums, where life carries on much as it does in the sea. That makes tidepools perfect places for you to discover what happens beneath the ocean.

You'll find that tidepool animals use a range of tricks to feed themselves. The flowerlike sea anemone has slender tentacles that trap and sting crabs. A barnacle sticks feathery feet out of its shell to kick floating food into its mouth. And a sea star opens clam shells—only a crack—then pokes its stomach, inside out, through its mouth and into the clam to eat!

INDEX

ACKNOWLEDGMENTS

Besides the support and enthusiasm of editor Elizabeth McLean and the gang at Annick Press and the creative design of Irvin Cheung, the author wishes to acknowledge the expertise and work of the American Society for Microbiology; William Amos, retired biologist; BBC news, science staff; Don Belt, "The World's Great Lake," *National Geographic Magazine*; Susan Binkley, Minnesota Department of Natural Resources; Linda Brennan, "Slime Time," *Ranger Rick Nature Magazine*; Bill Bryson, *A Short History of Nearly Everything*; Dr. Steven Businger, Department of Meteorology, University of Hawaii; Canadian Wildlife Service & Canadian Wildlife Federation; Connecticut Department of Environmental Protection; Cornell Laboratory of Ornithology; Wayne Crans, Rutgers University; Jerry Dennis, *The Bird in the Waterfall*; Bastiaan Drees and Mary Wicksten, Texas Agricultural Extension Service, Texas A&M University System; Wayland Drew, Don Baldwin, Alan Emery, Wayne McLaren, and Robert Collins, *The Nature of Fish*; Environment Canada; Beverly Fenn, Colorado Herpetological Society; Florida Museum of Natural History; Dr. Devon Hamilton, Ontario Science Centre; Dr. Keith C. Heidorn, The Weather Doctor; howstuffworks.com; Rob Hutchinson, Veterinary Entomology; Institute for Watershed Studies; Irkutsh State University; Dr. Karl Kruszelnicki, University of Sydney; Patricia Lucas, Kentucky IPM Program, University of Kentucky; Anne Maglia, Division of Herpetology, Natural History Museum,

University of Kansas; Joanna Marchant, "The Clouds Sailing Over Our Heads May Be Home to Thriving Communities of Microorganisms," *New Scientist Magazine*; Maryland Department of Natural Resources; Dr. Peter Merrett, British Arachnological Society; Minnesota Pollution Control Agency; John Mitchell, "Our Disappearing Wetlands," *National Geographic Magazine*; Montana State University; Muséum National d'Histoire Naturelle, Laboratoire de Paléontologie; National Museum of Natural History, Smithsonian Institute; National Oceanographic Data Center; news@nature.com; New Zealand Department of Conservation; Ohio State University Extension; Dr. Heather Proctor, University of Alberta; Herbert Ross, *A Textbook of Entomology*; United States Environmental Protection Agency; University of Arizona; University of California Berkeley, Museum of Paleontology; University of Kentucky, Entomology Department; University of Saskatchewan Extension Division; University of Wisconsin Sea Grant Institute; Tom Volk, Department of Biology, University of Wisconsin; Dr. Gilbert Waldbauer, *The Handy Bug Answer Book*; Washington University Medical School; Wisconsin Department of Natural Resources— and especially the clarification provided by Dr. Win Meijer, Conway Institute of Biomolecular and Biomedical Research, University College Dublin, and Dave Sherman, Ohio Department of Natural Resources, Division of Wildlife; and pronunciation advice offered by Aida Mustapic.

PHOTO CREDITS